KU-016-026

Contents

A Note About These Stories

These stories were written by Sir Arthur Conan Doyle (1859–1930).

The stories are about Sherlock Holmes and his friend, Dr Watson.

Sherlock Holmes is not a policeman. He is a private detective. People pay him to find things that are lost or stolen. Holmes likes to solve mysteries and catch criminals.

The stories were written about a time before telephones were in use. If someone wanted to send an important message quickly, they sent a telegram. Also, the money used in Britain was different. Today, in Britain, we use pounds and pence. In the 1890s, people used pounds, shillings and pence and there was also a large gold coin worth five pounds.

HEINEMANN ELT GUIDED READERS

ELEMENTARY LEVEL

SIR ARTHUR CONAN DOYLE

Silver Blaze
and Other Stories

Retold by Anne Collins

HEINEMANN ELT

ELEMENTARY LEVEL

Series Editor: John Milne

The Heinemann ELT Guided Readers provide a choice of enjoyable reading material for learners of English. The series is published at five levels – Starter, Beginner, Elementary, Intermediate and Upper. At **Elementary Level**, the control of content and language has the following main features:

Information Control

Stories have straightforward plots and a restricted number of main characters. Information which is vital to the understanding of the story is clearly presented and repeated when necessary. Difficult allusion and metaphor are avoided and cultural backgrounds are made explicit.

Structure Control

Students will meet those grammatical features which they have already been taught in their elementary course of studies. Other grammatical features occasionally occur with which the students may not be so familiar, but their use is made clear through context and reinforcement. This ensures that the reading as well as being enjoyable provides a continual learning situation for the students. Sentences are kept short – a maximum of two clauses in nearly all cases – and within sentences there is a balanced use of simple adverbial and adjectival phrases. Great care is taken with pronoun reference.

Vocabulary Control

At **Elementary Level** there is a limited use of a carefully controlled vocabulary of approximately 1,100 basic words. At the same time, students are given some opportunity to meet new or unfamiliar words in contexts where their meaning is obvious. The meaning of words introduced in this way is reinforced by repetition. Help is also given to the students in the form of vivid illustrations which are closely related to the text.

THE BLUE CARBUNCLE

1

A Hat and a Goose

It was two days after Christmas. I decided to visit my friend Sherlock Holmes, the famous private detective.

When I entered the sitting-room, Holmes was lying on the sofa. He was smoking his pipe. Beside the sofa was a chair. A hat was hanging from the back of the chair. The hat looked old and dirty.

Holmes was staring at the hat.

'Are you busy this morning, Holmes?' I asked.

'No, Watson,' said Holmes. 'I'm glad you've come. Look at this hat. It's very interesting.'

'Why is it interesting?' I asked. 'Who does the hat belong to?'

'I don't know,' replied Holmes. 'But Peterson, the porter who looks after this apartment, found it. He also found a goose with the hat.'

'A hat and a goose!' I cried. 'How strange. How did Peterson find these things?'

'The night before Christmas,' Holmes said, 'Peterson went to a party. After the party, he walked home along Tottenham Court Road. A tall man was walking in front of him. This man was carrying a large, white goose over his shoulder.

'Suddenly,' Holmes continued, 'a group of rough young men appeared. They tried to attack the tall man. Perhaps they wanted to steal the goose. The tall man raised his walking-stick.

But the stick hit a shop window behind him. The broken glass fell on the pavement with a loud crash.'

'The tall man became frightened,' Holmes went on. 'He dropped the goose and ran away. Peterson went towards the young men. When they saw him, they also ran away. Perhaps they thought Peterson was a policeman.'

'What did Peterson do then?' I asked.

'He brought the hat and the goose to me on Christmas morning,' replied Holmes. 'A label was tied to the goose's leg. This label said "For Mrs Henry Baker". And the initials "H.B." were inside the hat.'

'So the owner of the hat must be Mr Henry Baker,' I said. 'And the goose was probably a present for his wife. By the way, Holmes – where is the goose?'

'Peterson and his family are eating it now,' Holmes replied.

Suddenly the door opened and a man rushed in. It was Peterson. He was very excited.

'The goose, Mr Holmes! The goose!' he cried.

2

A Strange Mystery

We stared at Peterson in astonishment.

'What's happened to the goose?' asked Holmes.

'Look, sir!' said Peterson. 'See what my wife has found inside the goose.'

Peterson held out his hand. In the palm of his hand, I saw a beautiful, blue jewel. The jewel shone and sparkled with brilliant lights.

'But the stick hit a shop window behind him.'

'What is it Holmes?' I asked. 'Is it a diamond?'

Holmes leant forward excitedly.

'No, Watson,' he said. 'It isn't a diamond. It's the Blue Carbuncle.'

'The Blue Carbuncle!' I said. 'What's that?'

'A very famous, unusual jewel,' replied Holmes. 'It belongs to a rich lady, the Countess of Morcar. But it was stolen last week.'

Holmes got up and went over to his desk. He looked in a drawer and found a newspaper. The newspaper was five days old.

'Read this,' said Holmes.

JEWEL ROBBERY AT
THE HOTEL COSMOPOLITAN
BLUE CARBUNCLE STOLEN

The Countess of Morcar's famous jewel, the Blue Carbuncle, was stolen this afternoon. The robbery took place at the Hotel Cosmopolitan, where the Countess was staying.

The robbery was discovered by Mr James Ryder, under-manager of the hotel. Mr Ryder found that someone had broken into the Countess's room.

The Countess kept the Blue Carbuncle in a jewel-box in her desk. The jewel-box was empty and the Blue Carbuncle had disappeared.

'This is a very strange mystery,' said Holmes. 'We have found the Blue Carbuncle inside a goose! But how did it get there?'

Holmes thought for a few moments.

'We know the goose belonged to a man called Henry Baker,'

he went on. 'We must find Henry Baker at once. We must see if he knows anything about the Blue Carbuncle.'

'But how can we find Henry Baker?' I asked.

'We'll advertise in the newspaper,' replied Holmes.

He took a pen and some paper and wrote out this advertisement:

Found in Tottenham Court Road on Christmas Eve ~a goose and a black hat. Mr Henry Baker can have these things if he comes to 221B, Baker Street, at 6.30 this evening.

'Now Peterson,' said Holmes to the porter, 'please go to the newspaper advertising agency. I want this advertisement printed in all the evening newspapers. Then come back here. Also, take this money and buy another goose. I'll need a goose for Mr Henry Baker.'

3

Mr Henry Baker

When Peterson had gone, Holmes said, 'Watson, if Henry Baker comes this evening, we'll give him a simple test.'

'What kind of test?' I asked.

'A test to see if he knows anything about the Blue Carbuncle,' answered Holmes. 'But meanwhile we must wait.'

I had some work to do, so I went out. But at about half past six I returned to Baker Street. A tall man was waiting outside

Holmes's apartment. We went inside together.

'Good evening Watson,' said Holmes. 'And you, sir – are you Mr Henry Baker?'

'Yes,' said the man. 'I'm Henry Baker. I read your advertisement – the advertisement about the hat and the goose.'

'Please sit down, Mr Baker,' said Holmes. He pointed at the black hat on the chair. 'Is this your hat?'

'Yes,' said the man.

'Excellent!' cried Holmes. 'But I'm sorry about your goose. We had to eat it.'

'You've eaten it!' The man rose from his chair excitedly.

'Yes. We had to eat the goose before the meat went bad. But we've bought a fresh goose for you. It's over there on the desk. We still have the feathers, legs and head of your goose. Do you want to take these things?'

Henry Baker began to laugh.

'No, thank you,' he said. 'These things are no use to me. I'll be very happy to take the other goose. Thank you very much.'

'Good,' said Holmes. 'Well, here's your hat and your goose. By the way, the first goose was delicious. Where did you buy it?'

'Well,' replied Henry Baker, 'I got it from Mr Windigate, landlord of the Alpha Inn, near the British Museum. Mr Windigate ran a "goose club" for his customers.'

'What's a "goose club"?' I asked.

'Well,' replied Mr Henry Baker, 'a goose is very expensive, you know. And a goose club is a way of saving money to buy a goose at Christmas. Each member of the goose club paid Mr Windigate a few pence every week. Mr Windigate collected the money week by week. By Christmas, there was enough money to buy a goose for everybody in the club. Mr Windigate bought the geese. So each member of the club had a goose to eat on Christmas Day.'

When Henry Baker had gone, Holmes said, 'Well, Watson, Henry Baker knows nothing about the Blue Carbuncle. He wasn't interested in the goose he lost. He only wanted a goose to eat. He was happy to take the other goose.'

'So what do we do now?' I asked.

'Henry Baker told us his goose came from Mr Windigate of the Alpha Inn,' Holmes replied. 'Now we must go and see Mr Windigate. We must ask him some questions about this goose. Come on!'

4

The Goose Chase Begins

It was a cold, clear night and the stars were shining brightly. We walked quickly to the Alpha Inn, near the British Museum.

Inside the inn, a red-faced man was serving beer. The red-faced man was the landlord, Mr Windigate. We asked for two glasses of beer.

'I hope your beer is as good as your geese,' said Holmes.

'My geese?' said the landlord in surprise.

'Yes. A friend of mine, Mr Henry Baker, told me about your "goose club". He said your geese were excellent.'

'Oh, I see,' said Mr Windigate. 'But those geese weren't mine. I bought them from a salesman at Covent Garden Market.'

Holmes leant forward excitedly.

'Do you remember the salesman's name?' he asked.

'Yes,' replied Mr Windigate. 'It was Breckinridge.'

'Thank you very much,' said Holmes. 'Come on, Watson!'

We went outside into the street.

'Now, Watson,' said Holmes. 'We must find this salesman Breckinridge at Covent Garden Market. Windigate bought the geese from Breckinridge. So perhaps Breckinridge knows something about the Blue Carbuncle.'

We walked through many narrow streets. At last we reached Covent Garden. There were many stalls in the market place. I saw the name "Breckinridge" on one of the stalls.

A man was just closing up the shutters of the stall.

'Good evening,' said Holmes in a friendly voice. 'Are you Mr Breckinridge?'

'That's right,' said the man. 'What do you want?'

'Have you any geese?' asked Holmes.

'No,' said the man. 'I've sold all my geese.'

'That's a pity,' said Holmes. 'The landlord of the Alpha Inn, Mr Windigate, advised me to come to you. He said your geese were excellent. Where did you get them from?'

To my surprise, Breckinridge suddenly became very angry.

'I'm not telling you,' he said. 'People keep asking me questions about those geese. Why is everybody so interested in them?'

5

A Clever Bet

'I won't tell you anything,' repeated Breckinridge. 'Too many people are asking questions about those geese.'

'I'm not interested in anybody else,' said Holmes. 'But I'll make a bet with you. I bet you five pounds the geese came from a farm outside London. The best geese always come from farms in the country.'

'You're wrong,' said Breckinridge. 'The geese which went to the Alpha Inn didn't come from a farm in the country. They came from London.'

'I don't believe you,' said Holmes. 'I'm sure they came from the country.'

Breckinridge laughed.

'All right,' he said. 'I'll prove to you that the geese came from London.'

He took out two large books and opened one of them.

'This book contains a list of the people who sell me geese,' he said. 'The names in red ink are people who live in London. Read out the third name on the list.'

Holmes took the book and read, 'Mrs Oakshott, 117 Brixton Road. This name is written in red ink. So that means Mrs Oakshott lives in London.'

'That's right,' said Breckinridge. 'Now let's look in the other books. This second book shows the dates I bought the geese. Look at the date of December 22nd. What does it say beside this date?'

Holmes looked in the second book. He read, 'December 22nd. Bought from Mrs Oakshott – twenty-four geese at seven shillings and six pence each. Sold to Mr Windigate of the Alpha Inn.'

'There!' said Breckinridge. 'I was right. I bought the geese from Mrs Oakshott. Mrs Oakshott lives in London. So I've won the bet. Now give me my money.'

Holmes didn't say anything. He took a gold coin from his pocket and threw it down in front of Breckinridge.

Then we left.

6

An Interesting Meeting

A few yards away, we stopped under a lamp-post. Then we both began to laugh.

'You're very clever, Holmes,' I said. 'Breckinridge refused to tell you who sold him the geese. So you made a bet with him. But the bet was really a trick.'

'Yes,' said Holmes. 'I lost the bet. But I found out where the geese came from.'

Suddenly we heard angry voices behind us. A man was standing in front of Breckinridge's stall. This man was small with a sharp, pointed face. He was arguing loudly with Breckinridge.

'One of those geese was mine,' the man was saying. 'Tell me who you sold it to.'

'I'll tell you nothing!' shouted Breckinridge. 'Don't come back here again. Don't ask me any more questions about those geese. Now go away or I'll call the police!'

The man turned and ran off down the dark street.

'Come on, Watson,' said Holmes. 'Let's follow that man!'

We ran after the man. When we reached him, Holmes laid his hand on the man's shoulder. The man sprang round. His face was white with fear.

'Who are you? What do you want?' he whispered.

'Excuse me,' said Holmes, 'but I think you're interested in some geese. Or rather one special goose. A goose that Breckinridge bought from Mrs Oakshott of Brixton Road.'

'Oh sir,' said the man. 'I'm very interested in finding this goose. Can you help me?'

'Perhaps I can,' answered Holmes. 'But first you must tell

me your name.'

'My name is James Ryder,' said the man.

'James Ryder!' repeated Holmes. 'I know that name. Yes, I remember. It was in the newspaper story about the jewel robbery. You're the under-manager at the Hotel Cosmopolitan. The Blue Carbuncle was stolen from that hotel. Come with us, Mr Ryder. I have some questions to ask you!'

7

A Shock for Ryder

We got into a cab and drove back to Holmes's apartment in Baker Street.

'Now, Ryder,' said Holmes, 'I'll tell you what happened to your goose. It came here. But it was a most unusual bird. After it was dead, it laid an egg.'

'An egg?' said Ryder. 'I don't understand.'

'Well,' said Holmes, 'it was a beautiful blue egg. Look, I'll show you.'

Holmes went to his desk and took out a box. He unlocked the box and held up the Blue Carbuncle. The jewel shone like a cold, blue star in the room.

Ryder began to shake with fear. He held onto a chair to stop himself falling.

'We know everything, Ryder,' said Holmes quietly. 'We know you stole the Blue Carbuncle.'

Suddenly Ryder threw himself down on the carpet in front of Holmes. He started to cry.

'Please, please don't call the police,' he said. 'Think of my mother and father. They will die of shame if I go to prison. I have never stolen anything before. And I promise I'll never steal anything again.'

'Sit down,' said Holmes sternly. 'You must tell us everything. How did the jewel get into the goose? And how did the goose come to Covent Garden Market?'

'All right,' said Ryder. 'I'll tell you everything.'

8

James Ryder's Story

'I am under-manager at the Hotel Cosmopolitan,' said Ryder. 'The Countess of Morcar came to stay at the hotel and I became friendly with the Countess's maid. The maid told me the Countess owned a famous jewel. The jewel was called the Blue Carbuncle. The maid also told me where the jewel was kept. It was kept in a desk in the Countess's bedroom.'

'I decided to steal the Blue Carbuncle,' Ryder went on. 'One afternoon, I saw the Countess leave the hotel. I had keys to all the rooms in the hotel. I went into the Countess's bedroom and opened the desk. I found a jewel-box in the desk. Inside the jewel-box was the Blue Carbuncle.'

Ryder stopped talking for a moment. Then he continued with his story.

'I took out the jewel and left the empty jewel-box on the desk. I left the door of the Countess's room open. Then I called the police. The police came at once. I told them that someone had broken into the Countess's room. When the Countess returned, she found that the Blue Carbuncle was missing.'

'Then what happened?' asked Holmes.

'The police didn't think I was the thief,' Ryder went on. 'But I was getting very worried. The Blue Carbuncle was still in my pocket. If the police searched me, they would find it. I left the hotel as quickly as I could. I hurried to my sister's house. My sister lives in Brixton Road.'

'Just a moment,' said Holmes. 'Is your sister Mrs Oakshott – the lady who keeps geese for the market?'

'Yes,' said Ryder. 'When I arrived at her house, I still felt very worried. I went into her back yard to smoke my pipe. The yard was full of geese. My sister keeps geese and feeds them. She sells them to the market in Covent Garden. Suddenly I had a wonderful idea. I had to find a safe place to hide the Blue Carbuncle. Why not hide the jewel inside a goose? The police would never find it!

'I caught a large goose with a black mark on its tail,' Ryder continued. 'I opened its mouth and pushed the Blue Carbuncle inside. The goose swallowed the jewel! Then I went indoors to find my sister.

'I asked my sister if I could have a goose for Christmas,' Ryder went on. 'She told me to choose any goose I liked. So I caught the goose with the black mark on its tail. I killed it and took it home. Later that evening, I cut the goose open. But then I got a terrible shock. The Blue Carbuncle wasn't inside the goose! I ran back to my sister's house. But all the geese had disappeared!

' "Where have all the geese gone?" I cried.

' "To the market," answered my sister.

' "Were there two geese with black marks on their tails?" I asked.

' "Yes," said my sister. "They looked exactly the same."

' "Who did you sell the geese to?" I cried.

' "Breckinridge in Covent Garden," she said.

'I hurried to Covent Garden and found Breckinridge,'
continued Ryder. 'But he had sold all the geese. He wouldn't
tell me where they had gone. That's the truth. I stole the Blue
Carbuncle. But it didn't bring me any riches or happiness!'

Ryder hid his face in his hands and began to cry again.

There was a long silence. Then Holmes stood up and opened the door.

'Get out!' he said.

'What, sir?' said Ryder. 'Oh, thank you, sir!'

He rushed out of the room and down the stairs. We heard him running down the street.

'Why did you let Ryder go, Holmes?' I asked.

'I don't think this man will steal anything again,' answered Holmes. 'He's too frightened. And besides, Watson, it's Christmas. Christmas is a time for kindness and mercy.'

SILVER BLAZE

1

A Journey to Dartmoor

One morning, as we were having breakfast together, Sherlock Holmes said to me, 'Watson, I'm going to Dartmoor today to King's Pyland.'

I was not surprised by this news. I had been reading about King's Pyland in all the newspapers. King's Pyland was the name of some racing stables on Dartmoor, in the south-west of England.

Two days earlier, there had been a terrible crime at these racing stables. The trainer of a famous racehorse had been murdered. Also, the racehorse had disappeared. The name of the horse was Silver Blaze.

Holmes was sure to be interested in this crime. The terrible murder and the disappearance of the horse was a great mystery. Holmes loved to solve such mysteries.

So I was pleased that Holmes had decided to go to Dartmoor.

'I'll come with you, Holmes,' I said. 'Perhaps I can help.'

An hour later, we were in the train travelling towards Dartmoor.

'Watson,' said Holmes, 'let me tell you the facts about this case – everything that has happened so far.'

I leant back in my seat, smoking my cigar. Holmes began to talk and I listened.

2

The Stranger at King's Pyland

'Silver Blaze,' said Holmes, 'is an excellent racehorse. He has won many prizes for his owner, Colonel Ross. Whenever Silver Blaze runs in a race, people bet huge sums of money on him. They are sure he will win.

'In a few days' time,' continued Holmes, 'a famous race called The Wessex Cup will take place. Colonel Ross had entered Silver Blaze for this race. Many people have placed bets on Silver Blaze to win the Wessex Cup. No other horse has a chance of winning this race. Unless, of course, Silver Blaze does not enter the race.'

'So the only way to stop Silver Blaze winning the Wessex Cup,' I said, 'is to stop him from entering the race.'

'Exactly,' said Holmes. 'Silver Blaze has been guarded very carefully at King's Pyland. Silver Blaze's trainer was called John Straker. Straker was in charge of feeding and exercising the racehorses. Three stable-boys helped Straker with his work. Every night, one of these boys stayed awake. They guarded the horses in the stables.

'Last Monday evening,' went on Holmes, 'a stable-boy called Ned Hunter was on guard. The other two stable-boys were eating their supper in Straker's house. Straker lived with his wife in a house near the stables. About nine o'clock, a maid took Hunter his supper – a dish of curry. The night was very dark. So as she walked to the stables, the maid carried a lamp.

'Suddenly,' continued Holmes, 'a man stepped out of the shadows. He was about thirty years old and carried a heavy stick. He seemed very worried.

21

' "Can you tell me where I am?" he asked the maid.

' "Near the King's Pyland racing-stables," replied the girl.

' "How lucky!" cried the man. "I would like to speak to the stable-boy who is guarding Silver Blaze. If you take me to him,

I'll give you some money." '

Holmes continued his story, 'The stranger took a ten pound note out of his pocket. But the maid was frightened. She ran past the man towards the stables. Inside the stables, Ned Hunter was sitting at a table. She began to tell him about the stranger. But just then the man appeared again.

' "Good evening," said the stranger to Hunter. I want some information about Silver Blaze. If you answer my questions, I'll pay you well."

' "Go away or I'll get the guard-dog!" cried the boy. He ran to get a dog which was kept in the stables. But when he returned with the dog, the stranger had disappeared. Hunter waited until the other two stable-boys returned to the stables. He sent one of them to tell Straker about the stranger. Then he ate his supper.'

'What happened then?' I asked.

'When Straker heard about the stranger, he was worried,' Holmes continued. 'But he did not leave the house. However, about one o'clock in the morning, Mrs Straker awoke. Her husband was putting on his clothes. Straker said he was worried about the horses. He was going to the stables to see if they were all right. It was raining heavily. But Straker put on his coat and left the house.'

3

Death on the Moor

'Early next morning, Straker still hadn't returned,' went on Holmes. 'So Mrs Straker dressed and called the maid. Together the two women went to the stables. The stable-door was open. Inside, Ned Hunter was sleeping heavily. They shook him, but they could not wake him up. Silver Blaze and Straker had disappeared!'

Holmes paused for a few moments. Then he continued his story.

'Mrs Straker quickly woke the other two stable-boys. They slept in a room above the stables. Then everybody ran out onto the moor to look for Straker and the horse.'

'Did they find anything?' I asked.

'Yes,' replied Holmes. 'On the moor, they found Straker's overcoat hanging from a bush. They found Straker lying near this bush. He was dead. He had been hit on the head with a heavy weapon. There was also a deep cut on his leg.'

'Straker was holding a small knife in his right hand,' Holmes said. 'This knife was covered in blood. In his left hand, he was holding a black and red necktie. The maid remembered the necktie. The stranger had been wearing it the night before. When Hunter woke up he also remembered the necktie. Hunter was sure the stranger had drugged his supper. The man had put something in his food to make him fall asleep.'

'But what about Silver Blaze?' I asked.

'Straker's body was lying in soft, muddy ground,' said Holmes. 'The horse's hoofprints were everywhere in this mud. They could see the marks of the horse's feet all over the ground. But Silver Blaze had disappeared.

There was some of Hunter's supper left on the plate. A powerful drug was found in the curry. This drug made Hunter sleep heavily.'

'Do the police know who the murderer is?' I asked.

'Inspector Gregory is the police-officer in charge of the case,' replied Holmes. 'Inspector Gregory has found and arrested the man who visited King's Pyland on Monday night. This man is called Fitzroy Simpson. Simpson works in London as a bookmaker. If someone thinks a horse will win a race, they give Simpson money. They are betting on the horse winning the race. If the horse loses the race, Simpson keeps the money. A lot of people have bet on Silver Blaze winning the Wessex Cup.'

'So if Silver Blaze doesn't win the race,' I said, 'Fitzroy Simpson will have thousands of pounds.'

'Yes,' said Holmes. 'But Fitzroy Simpson says he didn't want to harm Silver Blaze. He only wanted to ask the stable-boy some questions about the horse.'

'What do the police think?' I asked.

'The police believe Simpson was planning to stop Silver Blaze running in the Wessex Cup. So he drugged the stable-boy and took the horse out of the stables. But the trainer, John Straker, followed him. A fight took place and Simpson hit Straker on the head with his stick. Straker fell dead. Then Simpson led Silver Blaze to a secret hiding-place. Or perhaps the horse ran away across the moor.

'That's what the police think, Watson,' said Holmes. 'When we reach Dartmoor, we'll see if their ideas are correct.'

4

The Drive to King's Pyland

It was evening when we reached Tavistock, the town nearest to King's Pyland.

Two men were waiting for us at the station. One was tall and fair with a beard. This was Inspector Gregory. The other was a small man. This was Colonel Ross, the owner of Silver Blaze.

'I'm very glad you've come, Mr Holmes,' said the Colonel.

'Has anything else happened?' asked Holmes.

'No,' replied the Inspector. 'But our carriage is waiting. Let's drive at once to King's Pyland.'

As we drove along, Inspector Gregory and Holmes talked. Their conversation was very interesting.

'I believe Fitzroy Simpson is the murderer,' said Inspector Gregory.

'But Simpson is from London,' said Holmes. 'He does not know Dartmoor. Where could he hide the horse?'

'The horse may be lying dead upon the moor,' replied Inspector Gregory. 'We're looking for him everywhere. We've searched all the other stables in the area.'

'I believe,' said Holmes, 'there's another racing stable very near King's Pyland.'

'Yes – Capleton Stables,' replied the Inspector. 'Silas Brown, the trainer at Capleton, also has a horse running in the Wessex Cup. But we've searched Capleton Stables. Silver Blaze isn't there.'

Holmes leant back in his seat. He was quiet for the rest of the journey. Soon we arrived at King's Pyland.

The moor stretched away in all directions. To the west lay a small group of buildings. This was the Capleton Stables.

Everybody except Holmes jumped out of the carriage. Holmes still leant back, staring at the sky. I knew he was thinking about the case.

Suddenly he jumped out of the carriage.

'Tell me, Inspector,' he said excitedly, 'did Straker have anything in his pockets when he died?'

'Yes,' replied Inspector Gregory. 'We found some things. They are all in the sitting-room in the house.'

'Then let's see them immediately,' said Holmes.

The Mystery Deepens

We went into Straker's house and sat round the table in the sitting-room. Inspector Gregory pointed to some things on the table. These things had been found in Straker's pockets.

There was a pipe and tobacco, some money, a few papers, a box of matches and a small, sharp knife.

'This knife is very unusual,' said Holmes. 'There's blood on it. This must be the knife found in Straker's hand.'

'This is a special knife used in medical operations,' I said.

'That's strange,' said Holmes. 'Why was Straker carrying a knife like this? And what are these papers?'

'They're bills,' replied Inspector Gregory. 'They're from a ladies' dress shop in London. But they do not have Straker's name on them. The bills have the name William Darbyshire on them. Mrs Straker says William Darbyshire was a friend of her husband.'

'But why was Straker carrying his friend's bills?' said Holmes. 'And look at them – these bills are for huge amounts of money. William Darbyshire's wife likes expensive clothes.

'Now let's go to the place where Straker died.'

All of us – Colonel Ross, the Inspector, Holmes and myself walked across the moor. We came to the place where Straker's body had been found. We saw the bush where his coat had been hung.

There were many prints in the mud round this bush – men's footprints and the prints of a horse's hoofs. Ho!mes examined the ground carefully.

'What's this?' he cried suddenly.

He held up a small matchstick. It was half-burnt and covered with mud.

Inspector Gregory looked annoyed.

'Why didn't I see that before?' he said.

'Because the match was hidden in the mud,' replied Holmes. 'I saw it because I was looking for it.'

Then Holmes stood up. He began to search the ground near the bushes.

'I think I'll go for a walk across the moor,' he said suddenly.

Colonel Ross looked at his watch impatiently. He turned

away from Holmes and talked to the Inspector.

'Inspector Gregory,' he said. 'I want your advice on an important matter. Shall I take Silver Blaze's name off the list of entries for the Wessex Cup?'

'Certainly not!' cried Holmes at once. 'Leave his name on the list. Silver Blaze will run in the race!'

6

On the Track of Silver Blaze

The Colonel and Inspector Gregory went back to King's Pyland. Holmes and I walked slowly across the moor. The sun was setting and it was getting dark.

'Watson,' said Holmes, 'let's guess what happened to the horse. Where did he go after Straker's death?

'Horses like to be with other horses. Silver Blaze would not run alone upon the moor. He would look for other horses. There are two stables near here – King's Pyland and Capleton. We know he didn't return to King's Pyland. But perhaps he is at Capleton.

'Let's walk towards Capleton, Watson,' Holmes said to me. 'Let's see if we can find any hoofmarks.'

A few minutes later, we came to some ground where the mud was soft and wet. In this mud, I saw clearly the hoofmarks of a horse.

'That's Silver Blaze!' cried Holmes excitedly. 'Let's follow the prints.'

We followed the prints and soon we saw Capleton Stables. To my surprise, another set of prints appeared beside the first – the footprints of a man.

'The horse was alone before!' I cried.

'Yes,' said Holmes. 'But somebody found him.'

The hoofprints and the footprints ended at the entrance to Capleton Stables. An angry-looking old man was standing at the gates. He was carrying a whip.

'What do you want?' he said angrily.

'I want to speak to Silas Brown, the trainer here at Capleton Stables,' said Holmes politely.

'I'm Silas Brown,' said the man. 'But I haven't time to talk to you. We don't like strangers here. Go away!'

Holmes leant forward and whispered something in Silas Brown's ear. Silas Brown's face turned red. 'That's a lie!' he shouted.

'Very well,' said Holmes. 'But shall we talk about it inside the house?'

'Oh, come in then,' said the man.

Holmes smiled and followed Silas Brown inside the house. I waited outside. About twenty minutes later, they came outside again.

Silas Brown now looked pale and afraid, and his hands shook.

'I'll do everything you say,' he whispered. 'You can trust me.'

'Very good,' said Holmes sternly. 'But don't make any mistakes.'

'I promise it will be there,' said Brown. 'Shall I change it first?'

Holmes thought for a moment then laughed.

'No,' he said. 'But . . . no tricks, or I'll tell the police everything. Come on, Watson!'

'He has the horse then?' I asked as we walked along.

'Yes,' replied Holmes. 'On Tuesday morning, Silas Brown found Silver Blaze running alone on the moor. He had an idea. This idea was to hide the horse at Capelton until after the Wessex Cup. Capleton stables also have a horse running in the race. If Silver Blaze doesn't run, Capleton's horse might win.'

'But Capleton Stables were searched,' I said.

'Oh, Silas Brown knows many tricks,' replied Holmes. 'And now, Watson, I'm going to play a little trick myself – on Colonel Ross.

'The Colonel has been impatient with me. Don't tell him we've found Silver Blaze.'

'Of course not,' I said. 'Anyway, we still have an important mystery to solve. Who killed John Straker?'

'No,' said Holmes. 'We're not going to arrest Straker's murderer. We're returning to London on the midnight train.'

7

We Return to London

I stared at Holmes in astonishment.

'What!' I cried. 'But we've been in Dartmoor for only a few hours. You've found Silver Blaze, but not John Straker's murderer. Why are we returning to London so soon?'

But Holmes said nothing more. Soon we arrived back at King's Pyland. The Colonel and Inspector Gregory were waiting there.

'We're returning to London on the midnight train,' said Holmes.

The Colonel stared coldly at Holmes. Clearly the Colonel did not think that Holmes could solve the mystery.

'So you can't find Silver Blaze or Straker's murderer,' he said.

'It's a difficult case,' replied Holmes. 'But I'm sure of one thing – Silver Blaze will run in the Wessex Cup. By the way, do you have a photograph of John Straker?'

Inspector Gregory took a photograph out of his pocket and handed it to Holmes.

'Excellent!' said Holmes. 'Come, Watson, let's return to Tavistock Station.'

'Wait,' said the Inspector. 'Can you give me any advice– anything to help with my investigation?'

'Well,' said Holmes. 'There's one important matter. The behaviour of the guard-dog at the stables. Its behaviour on the night of the murder was very strange.'

The Inspector looked puzzled.

'But the dog did nothing that night,' he said.

'That's why its behaviour was strange,' replied Holmes.

8

The Wessex Cup

Four days later, Holmes and I went to watch the race for the Wessex Cup.

At the racecourse we met Colonel Ross.

'I haven't seen my horse,' he said coldly to Holmes.

'Would you know your horse if you saw him?' asked Holmes.

'Of course,' replied the Colonel angrily. 'Silver Blaze has a white mark on his face and white patches on his front legs.'

There was a large notice-board beside the race-track. On this board were the names of the horses running in the Wessex Cup. I read the following six names:

LIST OF ENTRIES FOR "THE WESSEX CUP"
1. Mr Heath's *The Negro* (red cap, brown jacket)
2. Colonel Wardlaw's *Puglist* (pink cap, blue jacket)
3. Lord Backwater's *Desborough* (yellow cap, red jacket)
4. Duke of Balmoral's *Iris* (yellow cap, black jacket)
5. Lord Singleford's *Rasper* (purple cap, black sleeves)
6. Colonel Ross's *Silver Blaze* (black cap, red jacket)

Suddenly I saw the horses coming towards us. The race was about to start. I counted six horses.

'Look!' I cried. 'Six horses are going to race!'

'Six horses!' said the Colonel in astonishment. 'Is one of them Silver Blaze? I can't see him.'

The six horses passed by us and stood at the starting post. The sixth horse was large, powerful and black all over. Its rider – the jockey – was dressed in a black cap and a red jacket. These were the colours worn by King's Pyland jockeys.

'Those are my racing colours,' said the Colonel. 'But that horse isn't Silver Blaze. That horse has no white on his body.'

'Look!' said Holmes. 'The race has started. Here they come!'

The six horses were running very close together. But gradually the large, black horse came to the front. It overtook the others and finished first in the race.

'Congratulations, Colonel,' said Holmes. 'Your horse has won the Wessex Cup.'

'But I don't understand,' said the Colonel. 'Please, Mr Holmes, explain the mystery.'

Holmes laughed.

'All right,' he said. 'But first, let's go together and look at the horse. Ah, here he is.

'Look at the black colour on his face and front leg. That isn't the horse's own colour. The hair has been dyed. If you wash the horse, this dye will disappear. You'll find white hair underneath. you'll find he is Silver Blaze.'

'My dear sir, thank you,' said Colonel Ross. 'You've found my horse. But what about John Straker's murderer?'

'He is here,' said Holmes quietly.

Who Killed John Straker?

Colonel Ross and I stared at Holmes in astonishment. Then the Colonel's face went red.

'What do you mean?' he said angrily. 'Do you think I killed John Straker?'

Holmes laughed.

'No, Colonel,' he said. 'The murderer is behind you.'

Holmes stepped forward and laid his hand on the horse's neck. 'Silver Blaze!' we cried.

'Yes. Silver Blaze killed John Straker. But he did it to protect himself. Straker was trying to hurt him.'

Then Holmes told us how he had solved the mystery.

'The most important clue,' he said, 'was the stable-boy's supper on Monday evening. This supper was a dish of curry. You remember a drug was found in the curry.'

'Yes,' said the Colonel, 'but I still don't understand.'

'This drug has a very strong taste,' said Holmes. 'But so does curry. The curry hid the taste of the drug. The stable-boy did not notice the taste of the drug in the curry. He ate his supper and fell asleep.

'Fitzroy Simpson did not know that the stable boy was going to eat curry that evening. But Straker knew. It was easy for Straker to put a drug in the curry. He put the drug in the curry before the maid carried it out to the stable-boy.

'The second important clue,' continued Holmes, 'was the strange behaviour of the guard-dog in the night. The dog was kept in the stables. Someone came in and took out a horse. But the dog didn't make any noise. This shows that the dog knew the person who was taking the horse. That person was Straker.

John Straker took Silver Blaze out of the stables. But I wanted to find out why.

'You remember we found a knife in Straker's pocket. This knife was very unusual. It was a special knife used for medical operations.

'Straker was going to use the knife that night. He was going to make a tiny cut in Silver Blaze's leg. With this cut, the horse couldn't run well in the race. He wouldn't win the Wessex Cup.'

'But why did Straker want to harm Silver Blaze?' cried the Colonel.

'You remember the bills in Straker's pockets?' said Holmes. 'William Darbyshire's name was on those bills. I wanted to know more about William Darbyshire. It was strange that Straker had another man's bills in his pockets.

'The bills were from a ladies' dress shop in London. I took Straker's photograph to this dress shop. I showed the photograph to a shop assistant.

'The assistant knew the man in the photograph immediately. It was William Darbyshire. Darbyshire often came to the shop with a lady.

'I knew then that Straker was living a double life. He was John Straker in Dartmoor and William Darbyshire in London. He had a wife in Dartmoor and a girlfriend in London.

'The lady in London liked very expensive clothes. These clothes cost Straker a lot of money.'

'So Straker did not want Silver Blaze to win the race,' I said. 'He was hoping to make a lot of money. He was going to bet on Silver Blaze losing the race. And he was going to make sure that he won his bet.'

'Exactly,' said Holmes. 'That's why he took the horse out on the moor. He was going to cut the horse's leg.'

'But Silver Blaze became frightened. He kicked out and hit
Straker on the head.'

'But what about Fitzroy Simpson's necktie?' asked Inspector Gregory. 'We found it beside Straker's body.'

'I think that Simpson dropped his necktie earlier that evening,' replied Holmes. 'Straker found it and picked it up. Perhaps he was planning to tie the horse's leg with it.'

'But how did Straker die?' asked Colonel Ross.

'Straker took off his coat, lit a match and took out his knife,' answered Holmes. 'But Silver Blaze became frightened. He kicked out and hit Straker on the head. Straker fell dead. As he fell, the knife cut his own leg.'

'So the blood on the knife was Straker's own blood,' I said. 'Really, Holmes, it's wonderful how you've solved this mystery.'

'Yes,' said Colonel Ross. 'But I have one question. What happened to Silver Blaze?'

'He ran away,' said Holmes. 'But where he went to – that's a secret.'

THE SIX NAPOLEONS

1

A Visit from Lestrade

Inspector Lestrade often visited my friend, Sherlock Holmes. Lestrade was a police detective. He worked at Scotland Yard, the headquarters of the police in London.

Holmes was always interested in hearing about new police investigations. So he enjoyed Lestrade's visits very much.

One evening, Lestrade visited Holmes at his house in Baker Street, London.

'Some unusual things have been happening in London,' he told us. 'Perhaps they aren't important. But they are very strange.'

'What do you mean?' asked Holmes. 'What unusual things?'

'Well, you know those busts of Napoleon that are very popular,' began Lestrade.

'You mean the busts made of plaster?' I said.

'Yes,' replied Lestrade. 'They're plaster copies of the head of the Emperor Napoleon. Many people have them in their houses.'

'What about these busts?' asked Holmes impatiently. 'What's been happening to them?'

'Somebody in London is breaking them,' replied Lestrade. 'Three of these busts have been destroyed.'

'Perhaps someone hates Napoleon very much,' I said. 'Or perhaps it is the work of a madman.'

'Well,' said Lestrade, 'The man may be mad. But it is still a case for the police. The person who destroyed the busts is also a criminal. He broke into people's houses to steal the busts.'

Holmes leant forward in his chair.

'That's very interesting,' he said. 'Tell us all about it, Lestrade.'

2

Three Broken Napoleons

Lestrade took out his notebook and turned the pages.

'The first bust of Napoleon was broken four days ago,' he said, looking at his notebook. 'It happened at a shop in Kennington Road. The shop belongs to a man called Morse Hudson. Morse Hudson sells pictures and statues.

'Morse Hudson had a bust of Napoleon in the front of his shop. Hudson was in the back room. Suddenly he heard a loud crash from the front of the shop. At once he ran to the front. Nobody was there. But the bust of Napoleon was lying on the floor. It had been broken into pieces.

'Hudson rushed out into the street. But the street was empty.'

'What about the other busts?' asked Holmes.

Lestrade looked again at his notebook.

'The second bust was also broken in Kennington Road,' he said. 'A gentleman called Dr Barnicot lives in a house near Morse Hudson's shop. He is a doctor of medicine. Dr Barnicot has a surgery two miles away in Brixton Road to see his patients.

'Dr Barnicot admires Napoleon very much. He has many books and pictures about the French Emperor. And several days ago he bought two busts of Napoleon from Morse Hudson's shop.

'He put one of these busts in his house in Kennington Road. He put the other in his surgery in Brixton Road.'

'What happened then?' asked Holmes.

'When Dr Barnicot got up this morning,' continued Lestrade, 'he had a surprise. Someone had taken the bust outside and smashed it against the garden wall. It lay in pieces on the ground.'

Holmes rubbed his hands excitedly.

'Please go on,' he said.

'Later this morning,' said Lestrade, 'Dr Barnicot went to his surgery in Brixton Road. But the surgery window was open. Inside, his other bust of Napoleon lay in pieces on the floor. Somebody had smashed it during the night.'

'Tell me,' said Holmes, 'were Dr Barnicot's two busts the same as Morse Hudson's bust?'

'Yes,' said Lestrade, 'the sculptor who made the three busts made them from the same mould. So they looked exactly the same.'

'That's very interesting,' said Holmes. 'Well, Lestrade, please tell us if anything else happens.'

3

A Terrible Murder

Next morning, when I was getting dressed, there was a knock at my bedroom door. It was Holmes. He was holding a telegram.

'Read this telegram, Watson,' he said.

I took the telegram. This is what I read.

COME AT ONCE TO 131 PITT STREET,

KENSINGTON. LESTRADE.

'What's happened, Holmes?' I asked. 'Why has Lestrade sent this telegram?'

'Perhaps another bust of Napoleon has been broken,' replied Holmes. 'We must go to Pitt Street at once. Come on!'

When we arrived in Pitt Street, a huge crowd was standing outside Number 131. I wondered what had happened.

Lestrade was waiting inside the house. He showed us into the sitting-room. An old man was walking up and down. This man looked very upset.

'This is Mr Horace Harker, the owner of this house,' said Lestrade.

'What's happened here?' asked Holmes.

'It's about the Napoleon busts,' replied Lestrade. 'Another bust has been stolen. But this time something else has happened. Someone has been murdered.'

'Murdered!' we cried.

'Yes, Mr Holmes,' said Lestrade. 'Mr Harker, please tell these gentlemen what happened.'

'I had a bust of Napoleon in my sitting-room,' said Mr Harker. 'I bought it four months ago, from a shop called Harding Brothers.

'I am a writer,' said Harker, 'and I often work late at night. Last night, I was working upstairs in my study. Suddenly I heard a terrible cry. I rushed downstairs at once. The living room window was open and my bust of Napoleon had gone.

'I ran to the front door and opened it. Something was lying on the steps outside. It was the body of a man. His throat had been cut and there was blood everywhere. It was horrible. I shouted loudly for the police.'

'Who was the dead man?' I asked.

'We don't know yet,' said Lestrade. 'There was no name on his clothes. We found only two things in his pockets – a map of London and a photograph.'

We looked at the photograph. It was a picture of a very ugly man. The man looked like a monkey.

Holmes studied the photograph carefully.

'Where's the bust of Napoleon?' he asked.

'In the garden of a house near here,' replied Lestrade. 'But someone has smashed it into pieces.'

'Then let's go and see it,' said Holmes.

4

The Fourth Broken Napoleon

We went to the garden where the bust had been found. The pieces were lying everywhere on the grass.

'What do you notice about this house and garden?' asked Holmes.

'Well,' said Lestrade. 'The house is empty. Nobody lives here. So the thief came here to break the bust. He did not want anyone to hear him.'

'Yes,' said Holmes. 'But there is another empty house closer to Harker's house. The thief went past it first. Why didn't he break the bust there?'

'I don't know,' said Lestrade.

Holmes pointed to a street lamp above our heads.

'The light from that lamp shines into this garden,' he said. That's why the thief broke the bust here.'

'So the thief wanted to see what he was doing,' said Lestrade.

'Exactly,' said Holmes. 'Well, Lestrade, what are you going to do now?'

'The most important thing is to find out the name of the

dead man,' said Lestrade. 'We must find out who he was. We must find out what he was doing in Pitt Street last night. Then perhaps we will discover who killed him.'

'Well,' said Holmes, 'I have another idea. Let each of us work in our different ways. Let's meet later and compare our information.

'By the way, Lestrade,' continued Holmes, 'I would like to keep the photograph that you found in the dead man's pocket.'

Lestrade handed Holmes the photograph of the ugly man.

'Thank you,' said Holmes. 'Let's meet in my apartment at six o'clock this evening.'

5

A Visit to Gelder and Company

After Lestrade had gone, Holmes said, 'Watson, let's go to Morse Hudson's shop in Kennington Road. Remember, that was where the first bust of Napoleon was destroyed. Also, Morse Hudson sold two busts to Dr Barnicot.'

We arrived at Morse Hudson's shop about an hour later. Morse Hudson was a fat man with a red face.

'Yes,' he said. 'I did have three busts of Napoleon.'

'Where did you get them from?' asked Holmes.

'From a firm called Gelder and Company,' replied Morse Hudson. 'Gelder and Company made the Napoleon busts. They are very famous for making busts and statues. Gelder and Company are in Stepney, in the East End of London.'

'Thank you,' said Holmes. 'By the way, do you know this man?'

He showed Morse Hudson the photograph.

'Yes,' said Morse Hudson in surprise. 'That's Beppo.'

'Who's Beppo?' asked Holmes.

'Beppo is Italian. He worked here in my shop,' replied Hudson. 'But he left several days ago. I don't know where he is now.'

After we had left Morse Hudson, Holmes said, 'Watson, we must visit Gelder and Company – the firm which made the Napoleon busts.'

We drove eastwards through the streets of London to Stepney. Soon we found Gelder and Company. Outside, there was a large yard full of statues. Inside, about fifty men were busy working in a large room.

We spoke to the manager of the company. He answered Holmes's questions very politely.

'Six busts of Napoleon were made here at the same time,' he said. 'But they were not expensive. I don't understand why anyone wants to steal them.'

'Who made the busts?' asked Holmes.

'My Italian workmen made them. All our statues are made in this workroom. They are made of plaster. Then they are put outside to dry.'

'Morse Hudson bought three busts,' said Holmes. 'What happened to the other three?'

'We sold them to a shop in Kensington called Harding Brothers,' replied the manager.

Then Holmes took the photograph out of his pocket.

'Do you know this man?' he asked.

To my surprise, the manager became very angry.

'Yes,' he said. 'That's Beppo. Beppo used to work here.

We spoke to the manager of the company.

He was an excellent sculptor. He was very clever at making statues. But he brought trouble to my company. There was a fight in the street. Beppo tried to kill a man. This man was also Italian. The police followed Beppo and arrested him here. Beppo was sent to prison for a year.'

'When was Beppo arrested?' asked Holmes.

'Towards the end of May last year,' replied the manager.

'And when were the busts sold?'

'The busts were sold at the beginning of June.'

'So Beppo was arrested *before* the busts were sold,' said Holmes. 'I think that's important. Thank you very much.

'Let's go, Watson. We have work to do!'

6

Lestrade Has Some Information

'Where are we going now, Holmes?' I asked.

'To Harding Brothers – the shop in Kensington,' replied Holmes. 'Remember, Mr Horace Harker, the owner of the fourth Napoleon, bought his bust from there.

'The manager of Gelder and Company said that six busts of Napoleon were made. We know four of them have been destroyed. We must find out where the other two busts are.'

'What about this man, Beppo?' I asked. 'Do you think he's important?'

'Well,' replied Holmes, 'the dead man in Kensington was carrying Beppo's photograph. And Beppo used to work for Gelder and Company and also for Morse Hudson. I think he has something to do with this case.'

At Harding Brothers, we spoke to Mr Harding, the manager.

'I bought three Napoleon busts from Gelder and Company,' he said. 'But all of them have been sold.'

'Who bought the busts?' asked Holmes.

'Mr Horace Harker of Kensington bought one. The second was bought by Mr Josiah Brown of Laburnum Lodge, Laburnum Vale, Chiswick. The third was bought by Mr Sandeford of Reading.'

'Thank you,' said Holmes. 'By the way, do you have any Italians working for you?'

'Yes,' said Mr Harding.

'Are they able to find out who buys your goods?'

'Certainly,' said Mr Harding. 'The information is not secret. They can easily look in the sales book.'

We left Harding Brothers and returned to Baker Street. Lestrade was waiting for us. He seemed very excited.

'I have found out who the dead man is,' he said. 'I have identified him. His name is Pietro Venucci. He comes from Naples in Italy and is a member of the Mafia. He has committed many murders. He is a killer.

'I think that the man who killed Venucci is also Italian. Perhaps Venucci was following this man. Venucci saw him go into Horace Harker's House. He waited outside. When the man came out, Venucci attacked him. They had a fight and Venucci was killed.'

'Excellent, Lestrade!' said Holmes. 'But what about the busts?'

'The busts are not important,' replied Lestrade. 'The murder is important. Tomorrow, I'll go to the part of London where many Italians live. I'll find the murderer and arrest him.'

'But I think I can find the murderer tonight,' said Holmes.

'Tonight!' said Lestrade. 'Where?'

'At a house in Chiswick,' said Holmes. 'Come with us tonight, Lestrade. We'll arrest the murderer together.'

7

Beppo is Caught

Holmes was busy for the rest of the day. He was looking at old newspapers. I wondered what he was looking for.

At eleven o'clock that evening, Lestrade arrived. The three of us – Holmes, Lestrade and myself – drove to Chiswick.

I remembered Harding Brothers had sold a bust to a man who lived in Chiswick. Perhaps Holmes was expecting the thief to steal this bust tonight. Perhaps he was hoping to catch the thief.

We arrived outside a large, old house. I read the name, Laburnum Lodge, on the gate. This was the address Mr Harding had given us.

The house was very dark. There was a wooden fence all round the garden. We walked quietly into the garden and hid near the fence. Then we waited.

Suddenly the garden gate opened. Someone ran up the path to the house. Then we heard the noise of a window opening. A man was breaking into the house.

'Let's go to the open window,' whispered Lestrade. 'We'll catch the thief when he comes out.'

But before we moved, the man appeared again. He was carrying something large and white under his arm.

The man looked all around him. Then he put the large, white object on the grass.

Suddenly there was a noise. The man had broken the

object At once we rushed forward. We sprang on the man and held him.

I looked at the man's face. It was very ugly. It was the face of the man in the photograph.

But Holmes wasn't looking at the man. He was looking at the broken pieces of the white object on the grass. They were pieces of another Napoleon bust.

Holmes looked at each piece carefully. But all the pieces looked exactly the same.

Soon we were on our way back to the centre of London. Our prisoner didn't say a word. He looked wild and fierce. He stared at us angrily. Once, he tried to bite my hand.

At the police station, the man was searched. The police found a long knife in his coat. There was some blood on the knife. Perhaps he had killed Pietro Venucci with this knife.

'Well, Holmes,' said Lestrade. 'Thank you very much for your help. But I don't understand everything.'

'The investigation isn't finished yet,' replied Holmes. 'Come to my apartment at six o'clock tomorrow evening, Lestrade. I'll explain everything then.'

8

The Sixth Bust

When Lestrade arrived the following evening, he had learnt a lot about the prisoner. We knew many of these things already. We knew that the man's name was Beppo. We also knew he was Italian. We didn't know that he was a member of the Mafia.

Beppo was a clever sculptor and had made many beautiful statues. He came to London to work. He worked at Gelder and Company in Stepney.

But then Beppo started to steal things. He also tried to kill another Italian in London. He was sent to prison for a year.

Beppo had probably made the busts of Napoleon himself. But Lestrade didn't know why he wanted to destroy the busts.

Sherlock Holmes listened to Lestrade politely. But I was sure he was thinking about something else.

Suddenly we heard footsteps on the stairs.

A few minutes later, an old man entered the room. He was carrying a bag in his hand.

'Is Mr Sherlock Holmes here?' asked the old man.

Holmes smiled.

'I'm Sherlock Holmes. Are you Mr Sandeford of Reading?'

'Yes,' said the old man. 'You wrote to me about a bust of Napoleon. I was very surprised to receive your letter. How did you know that I own a bust of Napoleon?'

'Mr Harding of Harding Brothers gave me your address,' replied Holmes.

'I see,' said the old man. 'In your letter, Mr Holmes, you said you wanted to buy my bust. You said you would pay me ten pounds. But the bust was very cheap. I bought it for twelve shillings.'

'That doesn't matter,' said Holmes. 'I will pay you ten pounds. Here's the money.'

Holmes laid a ten pound note on the table.

Mr Sandeford opened his bag. He took out a bust of Napoleon and put it on the table.

As soon as Mr Sandeford had gone, Holmes rushed to the table. He picked up a stick and hit the bust. The bust broke into pieces. Holmes began to search excitedly among the pieces. Suddenly he gave a cry.

He held up a piece of the bust. The piece was white. But I saw something round and dark in the plaster.

'Gentlemen,' said Holmes. 'Let me show you a famous jewel. The famous Black Pearl of the Borgias!'

9

The Mystery is Explained

We stared at Holmes in astonishment.

'The Black Pearl was stolen over a year ago,' said Holmes. 'Do you remember the case, Lestrade?'

'Of course,' said Lestrade. 'The story was in all the newspapers. The police never found the thief. But how . . .?'

'The pearl belonged to an Italian princess who was visiting London,' said Holmes. 'The princess had a maid. The maid's name was Lucretia Venucci.'

'The name of the man Beppo murdered was Pietro Venucci,' I said.

'Exactly,' said Holmes. 'I'm sure Pietro Venucci was Lucretia Venucci's brother. The maid stole the pearl. Then she passed it to her brother.

'But somehow Beppo got the pearl from Venucci. We don't know how. Perhaps Venucci gave it to him to sell. Or perhaps he stole it from Venucci. Then Beppo got into a fight with another Italian.

'The police were chasing him. He knew he would be arrested. If the police searched him, they would find the jewel. Where could he hide it?

'Beppo was working at Gelder and Company,' went on Holmes. 'Six plaster busts of Napoleon were drying outside the workshop. Beppo was an excellent sculptor. He made a hole in the plaster of one of the busts and hid the pearl inside. It was a good hiding-place.

'But then Beppo was put in prison for a year. And while he was in prison, his six busts were sold to different people.'

'And all the busts looked the same,' I said. 'So he didn't know which bust the pearl was in.'

'Exactly,' said Holmes. 'When Beppo came out of prison, he had to look at all the busts. First, he went to Gelder and Company. He learnt that three busts had gone to Morse Hudson. The other three had gone to Harding Brothers.

'Then Beppo got a job with Morse Hudson. He was able to find three of the busts. But the pearl wasn't in any of them.

'Some Italians were working at Harding Brothers,' Holmes continued. 'They helped Beppo. They looked at the sales books. They told Beppo where the other busts were. Beppo went to find them. But Venucci was following him. Venucci had been looking for Beppo all over London. He had been showing people Beppo's photograph and asking where he was. At last he found Beppo, and followed him to Horace Harker's house. They fought and Venucci was killed.'

'How did you know there was something in one of the busts?' I asked.

'The thief carried the bust to a garden near a street lamp,' said Holmes. 'He needed the light of the lamp. Clearly he was looking for something. He broke the bust and then searched through the pieces.

'When I heard the name Venucci,' continued Holmes, 'I was sure I had seen the name before. Then I remembered the robbery of the Black Pearl. I found the story in an old newspaper. I saw the maid's name was also Venucci. Many people thought she had stolen the jewel.

'So I began to think about the Black Pearl. Was the thief looking for this pearl? There were still two busts left. One was in Chiswick and one was in Reading. Chiswick is nearer London than Reading. I believed that the thief would try to steal this bust first.

'So we went to Chiswick and caught Beppo,' said Holmes. 'But we did not find the Black Pearl. The last bust was in Reading. I wrote to Mr Sandeford in Reading and he brought the bust here. And so we found the Black Pearl.'

Lestrade and I were silent for a moment. Then we began to clap, like the audience at the end of a play. It was wonderful how Holmes had solved the mystery.

'Excellent, Holmes!' we said.

Points for Understanding

THE BLUE CARBUNCLE

1

1 When did Dr Watson visit Sherlock Holmes?
2 How had Peterson found a hat and a goose?
3 How did Holmes know the name of the man who had lost the hat and the goose?

2

1 Where had the Blue Carbuncle been found?
2 Who was the owner of the Blue Carbuncle?
3 Where had the robbery taken place?
4 Who had discovered the theft?
5 How had the jewel been stolen?
6 Why did Holmes want to find Henry Baker?
7 How did he plan to find him?

3

1 How did Holmes make sure that Henry Baker knew nothing about the Blue Carbuncle?
2 Why did Holmes want to meet Mr Windigate?

4

1 Why did Holmes and Watson go to Covent Garden Market?
2 Why did Breckinridge become very angry when Holmes asked him about his geese?

5

Why did Holmes make a bet with Breckinridge?

6

1 Why was Breckinridge shouting?
2 What did Holmes and Watson do when the man ran off?
3 What was the man's name?
4 Why did Holmes ask the man to go with him?

7

1 Why did Ryder shake with fear?
2 What did Ryder promise if Holmes did not call the police?
3 What did Holmes tell Ryder he must do?

8

1 Who told Ryder about the Blue Carbuncle?
2 Where did Ryder hide the Blue Carbuncle?
3 What went wrong with Ryder's plan?
4 Why did Holmes let Ryder go?

SILVER BLAZE

1

1 Who had been murdered at King's Pyland stables?
2 What had happened to Silver Blaze?

2

1 Who was the owner of Silver Blaze?
2 Why did people bet huge sums of money on Silver Blaze?
3 When would the Wessex Cup take place?
4 Who was John Straker?
5 What did Ned Hunter have for supper last Monday evening?
6 What did the strange man want?
7 What did he offer Ned Hunter?
8 Where was the dog kept?
9 Ned went to fetch the dog. What did the stranger do?
10 Where was John Straker going at one o'clock in the morning?

3

1 Was it easy to wake up Ned Hunter?
2 What had happened to John Straker and Silver Blaze?
3 Where did they find John Straker's overcoat?
4 Where was John Straker's body lying?
5 What had happened to John Straker?
6 Where was the deep cut?
7 What was John Straker holding in his left hand?
8 Who had been wearing the necktie?
9 Why was Holmes sure that Hunter's food had been drugged?
10 What had happened to Silver Blaze?
11 Why did Inspector Gregory arrest Fitzroy Simpson?

4

1 Who did Inspector Gregory believe was the murderer?
2 Did Holmes agree with Inspector Gregory?
3 Did the police find anything at Capleton Stables?
4 Why was Silas Brown interested in the Wessex Cup?
5 What things did Holmes want to see?

5

1 What was strange about the knife?
2 What name was on the bills found in Straker's pockets?
3 Where were the bills from?
4 What did Holmes find?
5 What did Holmes decide to do?
6 What did Holmes tell Colonel Ross to do about entering Silver Blaze for the Wessex Cup?

6

1 Where did Holmes find Silver Blaze?
2 How did Silas Brown look when Holmes and Watson left Capleton Stables?
3 What did Silas Brown promise to do?
4 Where was Holmes going on the midnight train?

7

1 Did Colonel Ross think Holmes could solve the case?
2 What was Holmes sure of?
3 What did Holmes ask Inspector Gregory to give him?
4 What was strange about the behaviour of the dog?

8

1 Why was Silver Blaze easy to recognize?
2 What was the name of the sixth horse running in the Wessex Cup?
3 What colours was its jockey wearing?
4 Why did Colonel Ross say the sixth horse was not Silver Blaze?
5 Which horse won the Wessex Cup?
6 How had Silver Blaze been changed?

9

1 Why had Silver Blaze killed John Straker?
2 Who knew what the stable-boy would have for supper?
3 Why was the behaviour of the dog an important clue?
4 What was John Straker planning to do to Silver Blaze?
5 Who was William Darbyshire?
6 How could John Straker win a large amount of money?
7 What did Holmes not tell Colonel Ross?

THE SIX NAPOLEONS

1

1 Who was Inspector Lestrade?
2 What unusual things were happening in London?
3 Why was it a matter for the police?

2

1 What happened in the shop belonging to Morse Hudson?
2 What happened to Dr Barnicot's two busts of Napoleon?
3 Did the three busts of Napoleon look the same?
4 What did Holmes ask Lestrade to do?

3

1 Why did Holmes and Watson go to 131 Pitt Street?
2 What was found in the dead man's pockets?
3 What did the man in the photograph look like?
4 Where was the bust of Napoleon found?
5 What had happened to it?

4

1 Why had the thief broken the bust under the street lamp?
2 What was Lestrade going to do?
3 What did Holmes ask Lestrade to give him?

5

1 Where had the busts been made?
2 Who was the man in the photograph?
3 What nationality was the man?
4 How many busts of Napoleon had been made by Gelder and Company?
5 Who had made the busts?
6 Where had the other three busts gone?
7 How had Beppo made trouble for the company?
8 When was Beppo arrested?
9 When were the busts of Napoleon sold?

6

1 Why did Holmes think Beppo was important?
2 Who had bought the second bust? Where did he live?
3 Who had bought the third bust? Where did he live?
4 Did any Italians work at Harding Brothers?
5 Would the workmen know who had bought the busts?
6 Who was the dead man?
7 What kind of man was he?
8 Where was Lestrade going to look for the murderer?
9 Where did Holmes think he would find the murderer?

7

1 How did Holmes spend the rest of the day?
2 Where did Holmes go to in Chiswick?
3 What happened there?
4 Who was the thief?
5 What did Holmes examine carefully?
6 Did he find anything?
7 What was found on the man at the police station?
8 Was the case finished?
9 What did Holmes ask Lestrade to do?

8

1 What had Lestrade found out about Beppo?
2 Did Lestrade know why Beppo was destroying the busts of Napoleon?
3 Why had Mr Sandeford come to visit Holmes?
4 How much did Holmes give Mr Sandeford for the bust?
5 What did Holmes do as soon as Mr Sandeford had left?
6 What did Holmes find among the broken pieces of the bust?

9

1 Who had stolen the Black Pearl?
2 Who did she pass it to?
3 Who had got hold of the pearl?
4 Why did Beppo hide the pearl?
5 Why did Beppo not know which bust the pearl was in?
6 Why did Beppo kill Venucci?
7 How did Holmes know there was something hidden in one of the busts?
8 How did Holmes know that the pearl was in the bust bought by Mr Sandeford?

A Christmas Carol *by Charles Dickens*
Riders of the Purple Sage *by Zane Grey*
The Canterville Ghost and Other Stories *by Oscar Wilde*
Lady Portia's Revenge and Other Stories *by David Evans*
The Picture of Dorian Gray *by Oscar Wilde*
Treasure Island *by Robert Louis Stevenson*
Road to Nowhere *by John Milne*
The Black Cat *by John Milne*
Don't Tell Me What To Do *by Michael Hardcastle*
The Runaways *by Victor Canning*
The Red Pony *by John Steinbeck*
The Goalkeeper's Revenge and Other Stories *by Bill Naughton*
The Stranger *by Norman Whitney*
The Promise *by R. L. Scott-Buccleuch*
The Man With No Name *by Evelyn Davies and Peter Town*
The Cleverest Person in the World *by Norman Whitney*
Claws *by John Landon*
Z for Zachariah *by Robert C. O'Brien*
Tales of Horror *by Bram Stoker*
Frankenstein *by Mary Shelley*
Silver Blaze and Other Stories *by Sir Arthur Conan Doyle*
Tales of Ten Worlds *by Arthur C. Clarke*
The Boy Who Was Afraid *by Armstrong Sperry*
Room 13 and Other Ghost Stories *by M. R. James*
The Narrow Path *by Francis Selormey*
The Woman in Black *by Susan Hill*

For further information on the full selection of
Readers at all five levels in the series, please refer
to the Heinemann ELT Readers catalogue.

Macmillan Heinemann English Language Teaching, Oxford

A division of Macmillan Publishers Limited

Companies and representatives throughout the world

ISBN 0 435 27193 8

Heinemann is a registered trade mark of Reed Educational & Professional Publishing Ltd

This retold version for Heinemann ELT Guided Readers
© Anne Collins 1987, 1992
First published 1987
Reprinted three times
This edition 1992

Illustrated by Kay Dixie
Typography by Adrian Hodgkins
Cover by Nick Hardcastle and Threefold Design
Typeset in 11.5/14.5 pt Goudy
by Joshua Associates Ltd, Oxford
Printed and bound in Spain by Mateu Cromo S.A.

99 00 10 9 8 7 6 5